dream therapy

dream therapy

INTERPRETATIONS AND INSIGHTS INTO THE POWER OF DREAMS

rosalind powell

southwater

This edition is published by Southwater

Southwater is an imprint of Anness Publishing Limited
Hermes House, 88-89 Blackfriars Road, London SE1 8HA
tel. (020) 7401 2077
fax (020) 7633 9499

Distributed in the UK by The Manning Partnership
251–253 London Road East, Batheaston, Bath BA1 7RL, UK
tel. (0044) 01225 852 727
fax (0044) 01225 852 852

Distributed in the USA by Anness Publishing Inc
27 West 20th Street, Suite 504, New York NY 10011
tel. 1 212 807 6739
fax 1 212 807 6813

Distributed in Australia by Sandstone Publishing
Unit 1, 360 Norton Street, Leichhardt
New South Wales 2040, Australia
tel. (0061) 2 9560 7888
fax (0061) 2 9560 7488

© 2000 Anness Publishing Limited

1 3 5 7 9 10 8 6 4 2

Publisher: Joanna Lorenz
Editor: Debra Mayhew
Designer: Ruth Hope
Illustrations by: Garry Walton

With thanks to Gina Stevens BSc(Hons)

Printed and bound in Singapore

Publisher's note:
The reader should not regard the recommendations, ideas and techniques expressed and
described in this book as substitutes for the advice of a qualified medical practitioner or
other qualified professional. Any use to which the recommendations, ideas and techniques
are put is at the reader's sole discretion and risk.

Contents

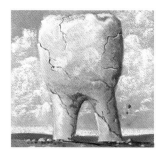

Dreaming
with Meaning

An Introduction to Dreaming

By their very nature dreams are ephemeral, and very often impossible to remember. If we do remember them it is often in the form of a confused series of images and feelings, but sometimes we have a dream which is so startlingly vivid that it stays with us for hours, or even days, afterwards.

There are countless theories as to why we dream, including a few to suggest that dreams are meaningless – simply the brain's way of disposing of the debris of the day. Yet to dismiss the significance of dreams and the role they play would be to ignore a part of our experience that is not only fascinating but can also be insightful and inspiring.

We have been intrigued by dreams throughout history and across different cultures. The Ancient Egyptians and Greeks slept in temples to encourage particular dreams, and various Native American tribes performed special dream rituals. We do not have to go to that

ABOVE A Midsummer Night's Dream *by Sir Joseph Noel Paton (1821–1901). In Shakespeare's play, Oberon casts a spell on Titania as she sleeps.*

extent to get in touch with our dream world, but we can learn to remember our dreams more clearly and understand them better. This in turn could lead to a greater understanding of ourselves and the people and influences in our lives.

Dream analysis isn't straightforward. We dream in a language of symbols and images, which need to be interpreted. This can sometimes be obvious, as with

LEFT *The dreams we have can be fanciful and impressionistic, as illustrated by* Le Chimère à L'île de Sarah Bernhardt (The chimera on the Island of Sarah Bernhardt) *by Georges Clairin (1843–1919).*

a dream about a supervisor at work who turns into a monster, but at other times we need to dig a little deeper to uncover a possible meaning. We must take into account what is happening in our waking life and how this relates to the dream, but some dreams may be about some inner process that has little obvious connection with other events. Once we begin to look at our dreams more closely, we may discover that themes or patterns begin to recur. We may even find that as a result of paying attention to our dreams, we dream more and remember the dreams more clearly. Every dream is unique, and the feelings of the dreamer are a crucial element in interpreting them.

Dreaming is by no means always a pleasant experience – many dreams are disturbing or even terrifying. But paying attention to these dreams can be particularly fruitful, as it can help us to understand and deal with life's problems.

Exploring dreams may reveal different aspects of ourselves, offer an interesting perspective on life, or fire our imagination and creative potential. They offer a key to a whole world of experience, which can become a lifelong adventure.

RIGHT The Dream of Philip II *by El Greco (1541-1614). Philip II was said to have experienced a religious vision which inspired him in his efforts to strengthen the Catholic Church.*

The History and Culture of Dreams

DREAMS HAVE ALWAYS held a great fascination for us. At different times, and in different cultures, they have been seen as warnings, prophecies or messages from the gods, and they have been bestowed with the power to solve problems, heal sickness and provide spiritual revelation. Shamans, priests and wise men were ancient dream therapists, revered figures in society who were relied upon to interpret dreams.

Methods of dream interpretation change, and we understand and use dreams in different ways, according to the beliefs of our society, but our desire to look for the significance in them has remained constant.

THE EGYPTIANS

The Ancient Egyptian civilization, which dates back as far as 4000 BC, was probably the first to develop a system of dream interpretation. The Egyptians understood dreams in terms of opposites: a happy dream meant that something bad was going to happen, while a nightmare was a sign of better days ahead.

Dreams were believed to contain messages from a variety of divinities or spirits, and herbal remedies would be taken

ABOVE *Imhotep was closely associated with healing and dreams. When ill, the Egyptians would visit a sanctuary where the gods would tell them in a dream what they must do to be healed.*

to encourage the good spirits and fend off the bad. Professional dream interpreters lived at these temples, and people would sleep there in the hope that the gods would send them a message through their dreams. This practice, known as "incubation", was widespread and is known to have existed in several ancient civilizations.

ABOVE *The dream stele of Thutmose IV records a particular dream: he was ordered by the gods to free the sphinx from the sand. In return they would help him to become king.*

ANCIENT GREECE

The Greeks were very interested in dreams and created a complex dream lore. They made a distinction between "true" and "false" dreams, breaking down the "true" or significant dreams into three categories:

- *the symbolic dream* – in which events appear as metaphors and cannot be understood without interpretation.

- *the vision dream* – seen as a pre-enactment of a future event.

- *the oracle dream* – in which a dream figure reveals what will or will not happen.

The Greek poet, Homer, used oracle dreams in his epic poems about the Trojan War, the *Iliad* and the *Odyssey*, both thought to have been written in the 8th century BC. In these epics, dreams often take the form of a visit from a dream figure (a god or a ghost), who appears at the head of the bed and delivers a message to the sleeper, and then usually disappears through a keyhole.

Dreams, in particular oracle dreams, were regarded as messages from the gods and were eagerly sought. Later, the practice of dream incubation (sleeping in temples to encourage significant dreams) was a highly organized activity. The Greeks regarded dreams as a source of healing; sick people in search of a cure would sleep at temples dedicated to Aesculapius, a magical healer-turned-god, who provided healing and medical advice in dreams.

One of the earliest dream-interpretation books was written by the Greek diviner and dream interpreter, Artemidorus, in the 2nd century AD. His five-volume work, the *Oneirocritica* ("The Interpretation of Dreams"), is both a dream dictionary and compilation of Greek dream lore, and includes his own observations on the subject. He was one of the first to realize the importance of taking the dreamer's personality and circumstances into account when interpreting a dream.

RIGHT *A Greek woman asleep, 2nd century BC. The Greeks developed a complex dream lore.*

THE BIBLE

There are countless examples of dreams in the Bible, which appear as one of the more common forms of communication with God. In Biblical times the Israelites were revered as dream interpreters by the Babylonians and Egyptians. One of the best-known was Joseph, whose story is told in the Book of Genesis. The eleventh and favourite child of Jacob, Joseph was hated by his brothers, who sold him into slavery in Egypt. There Joseph was asked by the Pharaoh to interpret two of his dreams and he accurately predicted seven years of hunger, but also recommended a plan of action that would save Egypt from famine. The Pharaoh was so impressed that he made Joseph his chief minister. Joseph was consequently honoured by his family, an event he had also foretold in a dream.

The belief that dreams were divinely inspired continued into the early centuries of Christianity, but slowly began

ABOVE *The Pharaoh dreams of seven thin and seven fat cows.*

to move away from dream interpretation as direct communication and prophecy. In the New Testament, dreams were seen as straightforward messages from God to the disciples. By the Middle Ages, however, it was believed that God's messages could only be received through the Church, thus ruling out the possibility of the ordinary believer receiving divine messages directly from God.

THE ABORIGINES

"Dreamtime" is the term used by the Australian Aborigines to describe the creation of the world by their great mythic ancestors. They believe that their ancestors (giants and animals) sprang

LEFT Jacob's Dream of the Ladder *by Luca Giordano, 1632–1705.*

from the earth, sea and sky in the Dreamtime to create the landscape, their giant steps forming mountain ranges, rocks and sacred sites. For centuries Aborigines have followed in their footsteps, as part of a spiritual journey or seasonal tribal migration. Each feature of the landscape, from waterhole to mountain, has meaning and is marked by songs, rituals and legends, which have to be re-enacted at certain times of the year to maintain the order of the land and retain links with the ancestors. Sometimes new information on a "dreaming track" presents itself in a dream, and a new ritual is created. There is little distinction made between waking and dreaming events, and many ceremonies are adopted directly from what has been seen in visions, or in sleep, by special individuals.

There are more than 500 distinct Aboriginal tribal groups in Australia, many of which have diverse explanations of dreams. The Dieri believe that a sleeper can be visited by the spirit of a dead person. The Narrang-ga believe that the spirit can leave the body during sleep and communicate with the spirits of others, or with the spirits of the dead who wander the bush, while the Japagalk believe that if someone is ill they can be helped by the visit of a dead friend in a dream.

ABOVE *To Aborigines, the landscape was created by Dreamtime, their name for the creation.*
BELOW *The Aboriginal Dreamtime spirit of Snake, called "Jaragba".*

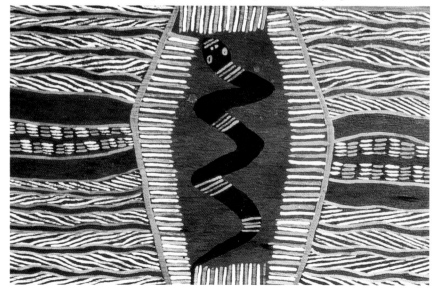

TIBETAN BUDDHISM

Buddhism is shaped by the philosophy that the world we experience is unreal or illusory, and the goal of religious or spiritual life is to "wake up" from the illusion. One way in which this "awakening" can take place is through the practice of yoga. In its original southern Asian form, the practice

LEFT *A Tibetan Buddhist meditating. Tibetan monks believe that they can control their dreams through yoga. This form of lucid dreaming helps the yogi to realize that the waking world, as well as the dreaming world, is a creation of the mind.*

encompasses a variety of exercises, both physical and spiritual, aimed at releasing the individual from the cycle of reincarnation. Although there are many different forms of Buddhism, it was Tibetan Buddhism – which was established in Tibet in 747 AD – that took the practice further by devising a form of yoga to control the dream state. This involves what is commonly known as lucid dreaming – the awareness that you are dreaming while in a dream state. Masters of Tibetan dream yoga are said to be able to pass in and out of sleep without even losing consciousness.

During sleep, the yogi (the person practising yoga) exercises control over the content and direction of their dream, and in so doing becomes aware of the fact that the dream world is transitory and can be manipulated by the power of the conscious mind. This, in turn, will help the yogi realize that the waking world, as well as the dreaming world, is a creation of the mind and therefore also illusory. It is also believed that controlling the dream state helps the yogi to determine where his or her consciousness goes after death – a major goal in schools of Tibetan Buddhism.

LEFT *In Buddhism, the goal of religious or spiritual life is to wake up from the illusion of the world we live in.*

THE NATIVE AMERICANS

According to the North American Indians, dreams are the most important experience in an individual's life. The meanings of dreams vary from tribe to tribe, but generally the influence of a dream is regarded as good or bad depending on the dream's content and its effect on the dreamer.

The Navaho usually interpret a dream in terms of its influence on the individual. If, for example, a dream has indicated illness then a curing ritual will take place. Dreams are divided into good or bad, and there are rituals to deal with the causes and results of bad dreams, the most common of which is to pray at sunrise. Some dreams are believed to cause sickness and require diagnosis and treatment. Death dreams tend to have standard interpretations. If, for example, a Navaho dreams he is dead, it means that he was visiting the spirits of the dead in the next world. If he shakes hands with the dead, it means that he is going to die. According to the Navaho, good dreams come true only once in a while, but bad dreams always come true.

The Mohave believe that dreams are the basis of everything in life. Good dreams indicate good luck, and bad dreams mean that

LEFT *The Navaho Indians believe that bad dreams always come true.*

ABOVE *A shaman wearing a wolf skin. By George Catlin:* Illustrations of the North American Indian. *Traditionally, shamans acquire their powers by dreaming.*

bad luck is around the corner. They also believe that shamans, or "medicine men", acquire their powers by dreaming and that they can enter their dreams at will. According to the Kamia of California and Mexico, dreams are better left to the young as old people risk dying during theirs.

The Psychology of Dreams

S CIENTIFIC RESEARCH has sought to reveal the process and mechanics of sleep and of dreams, rather than their meaning. Yet trying to decipher the meaning of dreams intrigues us the most.

In the past, as we have seen, people believed that dreams were brought to them by an external force and had some meaning beyond the purely personal. It wasn't until the advent of psychoanalysis at the end of the last century that our perspective changed and we understood that dreams, and their meaning, come from within the unconscious. Two of the most influential pioneers working in the field of dream analysis were Sigmund Freud and Carl Jung.

ABOVE *Freud's ground-breaking work on the analysis of dreams opened the door to many seeking access to the meaning of dreams.*

SIGMUND FREUD (1856–1939)

Freud believed that dreams were manifestations of repressed desires (usually sexual in nature) dating back to early childhood, and that the best way to explore and understand them was through psychoanalysis. The basis of Freud's psychoanalytic theory was the belief that most of our adult behaviour is determined by early childhood

LEFT *Sigmund Freud; his methods of free association and interpretation of dreams formed the basic techniques of psychoanalysis.*

experiences, especially sexual, and that if these experiences are painful we bury them in our unconscious mind. When we sleep, this repressed material enters our conscious mind in the form of dreams. However, since these desires are often shocking or threatening, they enter the conscious mind in a disguised, symbolic form. The symbols mask the true meaning of the dream, which can only be reached once they have been interpreted and understood.

FREE ASSOCIATION

The technique Freud used to reach this understanding and interpretation was "free association". He encouraged the patient, or dreamer, to express anything that came to mind, beginning with a symbol that had appeared in his dream. To try it, think of a symbol, then allow your mind to wander through any words that come into your head and see where the train of thought takes you, for example car – road – travel – holiday – Scotland – walks – healthy – refreshed.

Freud believed that this chain of association leads to the source of the unconscious problem or hidden meaning.

RIGHT The Desire and the Satisfaction *by Jan Theodore Toorop (1858–1928). Much of Freud's work centred on the idea of repressed sexuality and its appearance in our dreams under different guises.*

CARL JUNG (1875–1961)

Jung worked closely with Freud and was one of his early protégés until 1913, when their different approaches to dream analysis caused a rift between them. Like Freud, Jung believed that dreams could reveal the source of unconscious problems but he didn't believe that all dreams came from unconscious conflicts, or that the conflicts (and the symbols that represented them) were sexual. He believed that many symbols could only be interpreted and understood in relation to the dreamer's own experience, and could not be given fixed meanings. He also preferred to look at a series of dreams, rather than an individual dream, to see if a theme developed which could be important for the dreamer's personal growth.

Jung also believed that many dreams had more than a personal significance and contained symbols which, on the surface, appeared meaningless to the dreamer. These came from what he called the "collective unconscious" – a memory bank of thoughts, feelings and images shared by all humans from all cultures, which have meaning for everyone. This inherited memory bank manifests itself in universal symbols, images and stories, called "archetypes", which emerge repeatedly in fairy tales, myths, fantasies and religions and reflect our basic human desires and experiences.

For Jung, dream analysis was an invaluable tool for self-discovery and personal development rather than a method for unearthing past traumas.

DIRECT ASSOCIATION

Jung believed that thoughts and associations should always refer directly back to the symbol. To try this for yourself, write down the symbol on a piece of paper, for example – car, hold it in your mind, then write down all the associated ideas and images that come to you, constantly referring back to the original symbol, for example wheels – engine – speed – fast – control – power.

When you have exhausted this train of thought, move on to the next symbol and make a list for that one. You will find that certain themes will recur and certain symbols will become familiar. In time, you will learn to understand your own dream language.

FURTHER DEVELOPMENTS

There have been many developments in dream analysis since the work of Freud and Jung, but their theories on the unconscious and collective unconscious remain central to most contemporary

LEFT *Carl Jung worked closely with Freud until 1913, when he began to develop his own theories on dream interpretation.*

beliefs. Most modern interpreters and analysts agree that dreams often represent issues or desires about which the dreamer feels in conflict, and these often appear in disguise or are hidden beneath the surface. Dream analysis can help bring to the surface anxieties and concerns the dreamer may not have fully acknowledged, and can help people to confront emotions or conflicts they may have repressed.

Perhaps we should remember that the most important technique for interpreting dreams is simply to keep an open mind. The more open we are to possible explanations of our dreams, then the more likely we are to learn something from them. Simple appreciation of a dream can be just as enjoyable as chasing an exact interpretation – and it requires less hard work!

ABOVE *Many dream analysts today believe that your dreams represent conflicts that are present in your life. Dream analysis can help you to understand these anxieties.*

Why We Sleep and Dream

WHY DO WE SLEEP?

We spend a third of our lives asleep, and a quarter of that sleep time dreaming. Despite the major part that sleep, and dreaming, plays in our lives, there is not as yet a conclusive theory to explain why we sleep so much. Instead, there are only possible explanations as to why sleep is important to us, both mentally and physiologically – whether we need eight hours a night or if we are able to survive on just a few. Here are just some of the explanations offered to us:

- In terms of evolution, sleep is a strategy to conserve energy and reduce food consumption.

- On a physical level, it gives the body a chance to relax, re-charge and repair any damage. Our metabolism slows down, the immune system can concentrate on fighting infection and there is an increase in the production of growth hormone, responsible not only for growth but also for the renewal and repair of body tissue.

- On a mental level, we do less well if we are deprived of sleep. If we haven't slept well for two or three nights we are likely to suffer from poor concentration, memory failure and irritability.

SLEEP PATTERNS

Our sleep cycle is broken up into several distinct phases. Each of these is characterized by physiological activities such as eye movements and muscle tension, and the frequency of brain rhythms, or waves.

When we drop off to sleep we fall into what is known as "slow-wave" sleep, when the electrical activity of the brain slows down, together with our breathing and heart rate. Slow-wave sleep goes through four stages, with stage 1 at the earliest phase of sleep and stage 4 at the deepest, when the brainwaves are slowest. This is the time when it is most difficult to rouse someone.

After about 90 minutes of slow-wave sleep, Rapid Eye Movement (REM) sleep begins. The brainwaves speed up, heart and breathing rates increase, blood pressure rises and the eyes dart around behind closed lids. REM sleep is also called "dreaming sleep", as this is when

ABOVE *Our bodies have the chance to repair themselves during a good night's sleep.*

we have our most vivid dreams – or at least those that we remember.

We experience REM sleep at about 90-minute intervals four or five times during the course of the night, between periods of slow-wave sleep. Each phase of REM sleep becomes longer and more intense as the night continues from 15 minutes for the first phase up to 45 minutes for the last, which is often in the final hour of sleep before we wake up.

WHEN DO WE DREAM?

It was once thought that dreams only occurred during REM sleep, but the development of scientific study in the 1950s and the increased number of sleep laboratories have enabled researchers to study dreamers and brain activity during sleep more closely. Gradually it transpired that dreams occur throughout the night during periods of non-REM sleep, although they are less vivid and usually forgotten.

In the lighter phases of sleep (stages 1 and 2), dreams resemble the fleeting images and thoughts we might experience if we were simply lying in a quiet room allowing our minds to drift. Dreams from deeper sleep (stages 3 and 4) often take the form of fragmentary sensations, feelings and thoughts rather than images. When people are stirred

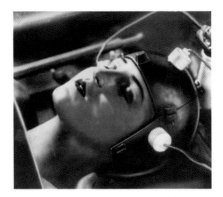

ABOVE *Our brainwaves can be monitored during sleep.*

from these deeper stages of slow-wave sleep they are often groggy, confused and unable to remember what they have dreamed.

In contrast, dreams during REM sleep have characters and storylines played out in a series of vivid images. Often we wake from REM sleep fully conscious and with clear memories of our dreams.

Our bodies also respond to the different types of dream experience. During slow-wave sleep we may twitch, talk or even sleepwalk, but during REM sleep we are virtually still. Although our brains remain active, we completely lose muscle tone which leaves us virtually paralysed. This means there is no danger of us physically acting out a dream, and also explains the sense of paralysis we often experience during a nightmare.

ABOVE *Insomnia affects us deeply. It can make us irritable and moody.*

WHY DO WE DREAM?

The eighteenth-century physician and naturalist "Erasmus Darwin" suggested that our dreams saved us from insanity by preventing us from having hallucinations in waking life.

His theory may not be that far-fetched. Studies have shown that if people are deprived of REM sleep (and their vivid dream worlds) they tend to become irritable and lack concentration. They try to catch up on the dreams they have missed as soon as they are allowed to sleep again by dreaming more than usual, even if this means having less non-REM sleep. This suggests that dreams are in some way necessary for our mental and emotional health. Other theories as to why we dream include:

- Dreaming is a sign that the brain is "ticking over" and interpreting signals from the outside world.

- Dreams are a form of catharsis, a way of resolving emotional crises.

- Dreams are a form of wish-fulfilment. They allow us to experience and fantasize about what we can't have in our waking lives.

- Dreams are a way for the brain to sift through information it has received during the day, and to dispose of any information it no longer needs through the dreams while storing information that may be useful. According to this theory, the brain will also consider ideas and grapple with problems.

ABOVE *Our dream worlds can be idealized versions of our "real" life.*
A Sleeping Beauty *by Richard Westall (1765–1836).*

WHY DO WE FORGET OUR DREAMS?

Even though we all have periods of REM sleep, some people claim never to dream. This is because they don't remember their dreams. But if dreams are so important to us, why do we so easily forget them?

About a quarter of our sleeping time is taken up with dreaming, which works out at approximately two hours a night. That is a lot of dreaming time to remember, especially if we only recall our dreams if we wake up during them or immediately afterwards. Most of us lead busy lives, and we wake up ready to get on with the day. Taking the time to think about what we may have been dreaming of during the night would seem a luxury that we cannot afford.

Another reason is probably because dreams are, by their nature, difficult to remember. They are frequently chaotic, confusing and without structure, and flash incoherently from one image to the next. Our memory of them tends to be partial and imprecise. We may remember only a tantalizing detail while the structure slips quietly away from us. It is always easier to remember dreams that are dramatic and colourful or those that have some personal significance.

RIGHT The Maiden *by Gustav Klimt (1862–1918). Our most memorable dreams are colourful and dramatic.*

Preparing for Sleep

A PEACEFUL, UNINTERRUPTED night's sleep will help create an environment in which dreams can flourish.

Make going to bed a pleasurable ritual, a time when you can put the day behind you and concentrate on the relaxing night ahead. If you are in the habit of going to bed late, retire earlier. The natural human sleep pattern is to sleep early and wake early, so don't waste time with late-night "pottering" or watching television.

ABOVE *A long soak in the bath can help you relax before going to bed.*

Think of your bedroom as a haven. Keep colours and lighting soft and warm, and tidy away clothes and clutter. Finally, try not to worry about the amount of sleep you are getting; our bodies usually make sure that we get all the sleep we need. However, if symptoms of insomnia persist, consult your doctor.

RELAXATION TECHNIQUES

A long soak in a warm bath has a soothing effect on the body, and can be further enhanced by using aromatherapy oils. Essential oils come in concentrated form, so you only need to add 5–10 drops to a full bathtub (no more than two drops for children); consult your doctor if you are pregnant. Experiment until you find the oils that work for you, but the following are traditionally considered the best for sleep:

- *lavender* – helps with insomnia, tension and tiredness.

- *sandalwood* – purifying, warming and soothing.

ABOVE *Aromatic oils can help you to sleep deeply. Candlelight will provide a relaxing atmosphere for a night-time bath.*

- *jasmine* – balancing, helps relieve stress and tiredness.

Bathing by candlelight will also make the occasion more relaxing and special.

The oils can be also effective if you use them in different ways, for example massage a few drops of lavender or camomile oil into the soles of your feet before going to bed, as both of these will act as a sedative. Put a few drops of lavender oil on your pillow and it will also help to induce sleep.

Avoid caffeine drinks such as coffee and tea at least an hour before retiring as they will probably keep you awake. Instead, have a bedtime drink such as hot milk with honey, camomile tea or lemon balm (a good restorative for the nervous system).

Once in bed, unwind physically by concentrating on the different parts of the body from your toes to your head: "I relax my toes, my toes are completely relaxed. I relax my calves, my calves are completely relaxed. I relax my thighs… I relax my hands… I relax my jaw… I relax my face…". Alternatively, tense and release each group of muscles starting at your toes and moving upwards through your calves, thighs, hands, arms, bottom, stomach, neck and face, giving your mouth, eyes, cheeks and eyebrows separate attention.

PREPARING TO DREAM

Before switching off the light, tell yourself that you will relax in body and mind, go to sleep quickly and sleep uninterrupted through to the morning. Or simply repeat to yourself,"I will remember my dreams". Say this as an affirmation – a positive and gentle way of telling yourself that you feel in control.

Just as essential oils can help us relax, certain herbs are historically thought to be conducive to dreaming.

ABOVE *Dream catchers, originating from the North American Indians, can catch bad dreams.*

Experiment with the following herbs by putting them in a small sachet and keeping it under the pillow:

- *mugwort* – said to aid dream recall and also to induce prophetic dreams.

- *rose* – has a relaxing smell and, like mugwort, is supposed to bring  prophetic dreams, especially those of a romantic nature.

- *rosemary* – useful for warding off nightmares and bringing restful sleep, also used if you want a particular question answered by your dreams.

Finally, hang a "dream-catcher' above the bed. Originating from the North American Indians, this is a net woven on a round frame and usually decorated with beads and feathers. The net is thought to catch bad dreams, which evaporate with the first rays of the morning sun, while the good dreams drift down to the sleeper below.

Dream Diary

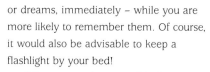

W E CANNOT BEGIN to understand our dreams until we begin to remember them. One of the most effective and interesting ways to achieve this is to keep a dream diary.

Begin now. Buy a notebook specifically for the purpose and keep it with a pen by your bed at all times. This means that even if you wake up in the middle of the night, you can scribble down the recollections of your dream,

or dreams, immediately – while you are more likely to remember them. Of course, it would also be advisable to keep a flashlight by your bed!

When you wake up, and before you start to write, close your eyes for a few seconds and try to recapture some of the images. Most dreams are a series of images, and remembering one could trigger a sequence. If you can't recall any images, try to remember how you were feeling as this, too, could trigger a fragment of a dream.

Now start writing. You could use the left-hand page of your notebook to record the dream, and the right-hand page for notes and comments. It is essential that you write your dream diary before you do anything else, so try

LEFT *Keeping a special notebook to jot down our dreams as soon as we awake helps us to spot patterns and recurring symbols.*

to make it a habit. The more conscious we are in our waking life, the less conscious we are of our dream world; any activity, such as having a shower or making a cup of coffee, will break that concentration and dissipate the dream. Try to include as much detail as possible, even the parts which don't seem to be relevant or don't make sense. Writing in the present tense will make the dream seem more immediate.

Once the bare bones of the dream have been recorded, you can begin to flesh them out. One approach is to look at the dream in categories, for example under the following headings:

- *significance* – is there a direct link between the dream and the day's events? Or does the dream reflect something from your past?

- *theme* – did the dream have a main theme running through it? Were you trying to escape from something? Is it a recurring dream?

- *setting* – where did the dream take place?

- *people* – make a list of the cast of characters.

- *feelings* – make a note of any emotions you experienced in the dream. Were you angry, scared, frustrated?

- *symbols* – did any objects figure prominently, for example a bird, tree or train?

- *words or phrases* – did any words or phrases in the dream jump out, or seem to have particular significance?

- *other notes* – was a colour, time of day or season relevant?

Remember to leave yourself space on the page for your own analysis. Put a date to the dream, and give it a title.

The longer you keep a dream diary, the more you will be able to make associations. Do certain objects make a regular appearance? Do you have a certain type of dream in times of stress? Can you spot patterns? You will find that you begin to gain an insight into your dream world, and into some of the events that influence your life. In time, you will also become more familiar with the images of the unconscious mind and will begin to recognize and understand your own symbols.

RIGHT *Use illustrations as well as text to bring your dream diary to life.*

MONDAY 1

Recurring dream.

Oppressive atmosphere - stormy weather.

Strong sense of the colour purple all around.

Feeling of alienation. No familiar faces - all strangers. Looked odd.

Driving along a long, long road. Feeling that I was late for something. Kept thinking I would see my destination over the next hill, but when I got to the top there was just more road spread out beyond. Felt panicky and stressed. Kept passing people hitch-hiking but no time to pick them up. Just before I woke up I saw the sea glinting on the horizon. Felt better. Then a fish flew past the windscreen. Made me feel happy.

Analyzing Your Dreams

DREAMS ARE MADE UP from our own thoughts and experiences, so our interpretation of them can only be personal and subjective. Other people can guide us through them or make suggestions, but only we have the knowledge about our life and experiences that is needed.

Once we learn how to understand and appreciate our dreams, we can use them to help us look at things in a different way, to further our self-development and, if not to solve a problem, then at least make us confront or assess it. Sadly, much of what we dream about is likely to be negative rather than positive. Happy emotions in dreams are less common and dreams are often about conflict, usually about conflicts that are currently affecting our lives. But this is not necessarily a bad thing: a dream can often make us confront a problem that we may be avoiding or refusing to acknowledge.

Although some of the content of our dreams may be familiar in many ways (they deal with people we know, in places we recognize and are about issues that concern us), the context can be entirely unfamiliar, with a muddled story presented in a series of surreal circumstances.

Most dreams exist on two levels. The surface level is made up of the people, events, sights and sounds of the dream. This will probably include fragments from the day – a person you have seen or met, or something you have been thinking about. The second, deeper level holds the meaning of the dream and what it is trying to express. However, not all dreams have meaning – they may well be just a regurgitation of images and thoughts from the day. But with time, and by keeping a dream diary, you will

ABOVE Christ's Troubled Sleep *from Milton's* Paradise Lost. *Illustration by William Blake (1757–1827). Sometimes a dream about conflict can make us confront a problem.*

be able to identify your significant dreams, the ones that could be interesting or useful to look at.

THE LANGUAGE OF DREAMS

The most indecipherable, and fascinating, aspect of dreams is the language they use to convey a message or meaning. It is in the form of metaphor and symbol which, like a foreign language, needs to be translated and interpreted.

There are a number of theories as to why the unconscious mind should want, or need, to convey information to our conscious mind in symbolic form. One is that the message is something we are not ready to hear, so if it is presented to us in an incomprehensible way we can easily dismiss it. Freud believed that symbols protect us from the underlying message, which is often so disturbing that it would wake us up and upset us if it was presented more clearly. Alternatively, the fact that the message is strange may force us to look at it more closely, and having to decipher and decode a dream could make us feel that we were "solving" a puzzle. Another theory is that we can only handle information in a limited way and that symbols and metaphors are actually an economical way in which to present the information.

Many symbols have been given common, universal meanings. These

ABOVE *We dream in a language of symbols and metaphors that we have to decipher.*

meanings are useful as a guideline, so long as you remember that these symbols may mean something different to you. For example, fire is said to symbolize anger but you may have a phobia about fire. Drowning is said to symbolize a fear of being engulfed by an unexpressed, unconscious need, but maybe you have a fear of water, or are learning how to swim. It is often the feeling attached to the symbol, rather than the symbol itself, that is significant.

METHODS OF ANALYSIS

Once you have started your dream diary, you will have the material at hand for analysis. The first step is to decide whether a particular dream is worth studying more closely. Is it simply throwing up an event from the day, such as a shopping excursion, which is neither interesting or useful? Or does it have some greater resonance, a feeling that stays with you or an event that seems important? One way of assessing your dream would be to look at some of the categories you have already used in your diary:

Setting Is it somewhere you have been to recently, or in the past? How does it make you feel? Try to think of words to describe it. For example, if you dreamt you were back at school, the words might be "young, teacher, learning, test". If you dream you are being tested, perhaps you feel pressurized when awake.

People Are they people you know? If so, what role do they play in your life? Or are they figures you have not met before?

Again, try and think of words to describe them. For example, you may have dreamt of a child, whom you describe as "young, sweet, helpless, crying". Does this say anything about how you are feeling at the moment? Do you long to return to your childhood? Or do you feel vulnerable in your waking life?

Feelings How did you feel during your dream? How did you feel after it? Have you felt a lot like this recently, for example, angry, frustrated or stressed? Emotions expressed in dreams can give us clues about our emotional state when we are awake.

ABOVE The Fall of Icarus *by Carlo Saraceni (1579–1620).*
Use myths, fairy tales and folklore to help you decipher your dreams.

EXPLORING SYMBOLS

The best way to try to unravel a dream is to explore and interpret the symbols within it. You will be bombarded by images, so try to select symbolic ones that seem important and leave a lasting impression. Symbols can appear in many forms and guises – not just as objects but as people, colours, numbers, even words. Some of the following techniques may be useful in trying to decipher what your symbols mean to you:

- *using a dictionary* – looking up the definition of a word will sometimes trigger different associations.

- *using a dream dictionary* – there are plenty of dream dictionaries to choose from and they will give you some idea what your symbols mean, or could lead to other ideas. Don't take their meanings as definitive, as symbols can mean different things to different people.

- *drawing your dream* – sometimes doodling elements of a dream can give you fresh insights.

- *explaining your dream to someone* – putting a dream into words can bring out different aspects, and the person you are recounting it to may contribute ideas of their own.

ABOVE *Explaining your dream to a friend can clarify your thoughts – and they can add theirs.*

- *looking at myths, folklore or fairy tales* – some symbols, such as a snake, witch and dragon, are dominant in stories. Perhaps a symbol you have dreamt of has played a role in a story or myth, which may give you a new insight.

- *free association* – this was the method favoured by Freud for dream interpretation. Think of the symbol, then allow your mind to wander through any words that come into your head and see where the train of thought takes you.

- *direct association* – this was Jung's preferred method of interpretation. Jung believed that thoughts and associations should always refer directly back to the symbol. Think of a symbol then, holding it in your mind, write down all the associated ideas and images that come to you. When you have exhausted this train of thought, move on to the next symbol. You will find that certain themes recur and certain symbols become familiar. In time, you will learn to understand your own dream language.

Controlling Your Dreams

THERE ARE METHODS to help us remember and interpret our dreams, but can we take the process one stage further and control them? The answer is that to a degree, and with time, practice and patience, we can.

DREAM INCUBATION

This involves actively generating a desired dream and has been widely practised throughout history, particularly in ancient civilizations. Modern methods to seek a particular dream tend to be different to those practised by the Ancient Egyptians or Greeks – we cannot sleep in temples, lie on the skins of sacred animals or hide away in sacred places, nor are we likely to call on the gods to suggest cures for an illness. However, we can try to guide our dreams in a way that will help us solve problems, generate ideas, make decisions or simply have a bit of fun.

The following are a few techniques that could help you dream about a chosen subject, person, time or place.

ABOVE *Studying a photograph can help us to dream of a person or a place.*

ABOVE *Looking in the mirror before sleeping could make you the subject of your dream.*

PSYCHIC SUGGESTION

Consider carefully what it is you hope to achieve from a dream, and write down what you would like to learn from it. Before going to bed, immerse yourself in the subject/person/place you wish to dream about:

- *a person* – look at photographs of that person, think about their character, try and remember times you have shared together.

- *a place* — look at photographs or objects from the place, or if you have visited it try to remember the time you spent there.

- *health* – pamper yourself with a bath, study your body in the mirror, think about it and how you might be able to look after it.

- *a relationship* – think about the other person, the times you have shared or

ABOVE *Using a positive affirmation can help you to dream about a chosen subject, for example, a real or desired surfing holiday.*

ABOVE *Write down your affirmation sentence. Repeat it to yourself at night.*

the direction in which you want the relationship to go or how you might change or improve it.

POSITIVE AFFIRMATION

A short, upbeat sentence can help your mind work in a constructive way. It should:

- be in the present tense

- be in the first person

- include your name

- be short and easy to remember

You can use positive affirmation to decide the subject matter of your dream, for example "I, Jo, will dream tonight about surfing in Cornwall", or to help concentrate your mind on finding the solution to a particular problem. If you are using it for the latter, make sure you

focus on the positive outcome and not negatively on the problem itself, for example "I, Jo, will cope with my workload tomorrow", rather than "I, Jo, will not get stressed out and feel under pressure tomorrow".

Your affirmation sentence can be written down or spoken. Repeat it regularly during the day, and when in bed repeat it to yourself to the rhythm of your breathing.

VISUALIZING YOUR DREAM

Visualization is a form of daydreaming, that can help bring about a desired mental state. Once you are in bed and feeling relaxed, empty your mind. Now, think as clearly as you can about the end result you wish to achieve from your dream, such as the solution to a practical problem or relationship dilemma. Now try to picture in your mind how you would behave and feel if the problem was resolved – relaxed, more confident and less anxious. Try to be as detailed as possible in your imaginings, then let your unconscious mind mull it over while you are asleep.

ABOVE *Before going to sleep, think carefully about what it is you would like to dream.*

DREAM MEETINGS

It is possible to have a shared dream experience with a friend or partner. This can either entail meeting in a dream or sharing the same dream, such as dreaming separately about the same event. Most people practised in the art of mutual dreaming, however, aspire to actually meet in their dreams.

First decide who you are going to meet or share a dream with. People who are emotionally close usually have the best results as they share many of their waking experiences together, which can provide them with the dream's subject matter. Use the following as a guide:

- Once you have decided on the night you want to share your dream, choose your mutual destination – a pleasant place, perhaps somewhere you have both been to together so that it is familiar to both of you and easier for you both to visualize.

ABOVE *If you are not sharing a bed with your potential dream partner, the telephone is always there to help!*

- Visualize the scene and describe it to your dream partner, telling each other what you envisage in much detail.

- Decide to meet there at a set time. Be very specific about the arrangements and rehearse them a few times before you go to sleep.

- In the morning, tell each other your dreams as soon as possible. Dream recall is very important so that you can make accurate comparisons. Sometimes these will not be immediately obvious, for example if you both dreamt in symbols, you will need to decipher the meaning of the symbols first to see if they compare.

The most important aspect of attempting dream meetings is patience – if at first you don't succeed in making any connections, then try again. Practical considerations also play a part and it is obviously easier to discuss your dream plans and compare notes if you share the same bed as your chosen dream partner. However, there is always the telephone.

BELOW *Mutual dreaming is where we share a dream experience with a friend, either by meeting them in a dream or sharing the same dream with them.*

LUCID DREAMING

A lucid dream is one in which the dreamer is aware that he or she is dreaming. Experienced lucid dreamers can consciously manipulate the dream's content – they can think and reason, make decisions and act on them. Not everybody can have lucid dreams easily, but it is possible to learn.

The term "lucid dreaming" was first coined by the Dutch physician Frederik Van Eeden, who began to study his own dreams in 1896. It has only been accepted and studied relatively recently, after dream researchers discovered solid evidence that lucid dreamers not only dream vividly but are also aware that they are dreaming.

ABOVE The Dream *by Henri Rousseau.*
Lucid dreamers are aware that they are dreaming.

Lucid dreamers are usually alerted to the fact that they are dreaming by an illogical or inaccurate trigger, for example, bumping into someone they know who is dead, or flying from a tall building. Sometimes it can be an emotional trigger such as fear or anxiety. Nightmares often lead to a period of lucidity, that fleeting sense of relief when you realize that the horrible scenario you are experiencing is just a dream.

Is there any point in being able to dream lucidly? Tibetan Buddhists, as we have seen earlier, believe that lucid dreams are a way of preparing for the afterlife, an environment similar to the dream world. Some masters of Tibetan yoga are said to be able to pass in and out of sleep without even losing consciousness.

A high proportion of our ordinary dreams (some people have estimated it as high as two-thirds) have unpleasant elements. We often dream of being attacked or chased, or of falling from heights, which makes us feel scared, anxious or miserable. Lucid dreams, however, rarely focus on unpleasant events because if a dream is frightening, lucid dreamers can detach themselves with the thought, "This is only a dream".

If you are aware that you are dreaming, you could, in theory, be able to change the course of the dream's events.

You could decide where you wanted to go, what you wanted to do and who you wanted to meet. You could even decide to confront fears by facing the monster chasing you rather than running away from it. Or you could just decide to entertain yourself.

If you want to develop the skill of lucid dreaming, you first have to be able to recognize that you are dreaming. There are certain things you can do to help raise this awareness:

- Ask yourself the question "Am I dreaming?" during the day when you are awake and just before you go to bed. This will make the question a constant presence in your thoughts and more likely to occur to you during your dreams.

- As well as checking whether or not you are asleep, check the physical reality around you. Is there anything strange or surreal about your surroundings? Can you float above the ground? Have you shrunk in size? The idea is that you make the same checks while you are asleep, and so come to realize when events are happening in a dream.

- Try to maintain a level of mental alertness while falling asleep. Stephen LaBerge, the Director of the Lucidity Institute in California, suggests counting sheep or reciting the 12 times table. This exercise should enable you to retain your awareness during the transition between wakefulness and sleep, with the aim that at some point you will actually become aware that you are dreaming.

- Repeat a positive affirmation before you go to sleep, such as "Tonight I will be consciously aware that I am dreaming".

There is an element of control with lucid dreaming, but we are still restricted by our own expectations and limitations. We can direct the dream to a certain extent, but we cannot completely control it. For example, once we know we are dreaming, we could decide to visit a tropical island but we won't know what it is like until we get there. On the whole, dreamers have to accept the basic scenario or concept of a dream, allowing it to evolve while exercising some control over their own actions or reactions. Exerting too much control could also wake you up!

RIGHT
17th-century icon painting of Saint George, the Patron Saint of England. Lucid dreaming allows us to confront fears and chase away monsters.

Nightmares

THESE ARE THE DREAMS we tend to remember the most. This may have something to do with the fact that we have them so often – one study estimated that one in 20 people has a nightmare at least once a week.

Our dreams are more often negative than positive, and anxiety is the most common dream emotion. Nightmares are laden with varying degrees of anxiety, from mild worry to blind panic. It is the feeling a nightmare evokes, rather than the dream itself, that upsets us and informs us that we have had an unpleasant dream experience. In extreme cases, we may even wake up with physical symptoms such as sweating or a pounding heart.

Certain physiological factors can trigger bad dreams. Eating rich food before going to bed can lead to indigestion and disturb the quality of our sleep; heavy drinkers who give up alcohol may suffer frightening dreams for a while afterwards; and certain drugs, such as beta-blockers, can increase the frequency of bad dreams. The strongest trigger, however, is psychological. If we are worried, concerned or miserable about something during the day, then these feelings will prey on our mind at night. They are reflected in common dream scenarios, which are not so much dramatic as mildly disturbing – taking a test; discovering a loved one in the arms of another; being inappropriately dressed at a social gathering, or ignored at a party; running but not moving. More dramatic common nightmares include being chased by something or somebody; trying and failing to get somewhere; exams, tests or interviews that go horribly wrong, or for which you are unprepared; experiencing or witnessing violence; being strangled or suffocated; feeling paralyzed but being unable to move or escape.

Some people go through their dream lives relatively unscathed, having very few nightmares. So why is it that some of us suffer from them more than others? Dream studies have suggested that those who are more prone to nightmares are

ABOVE Tartini's Dream *by Giuseppe Tartini (1692–1770).*
The artist experiences his anxieties in dream form.

ABOVE *Nightmares can represent your worst possible fears.*

"thin-skinned"' – they are sensitive, apprehensive and suffer a high level of tension in their waking lives. There also appears to be a link between types of personalities and types of nightmares, for example, ambitious high-achievers are said to have more fantastic, dramatic nightmares. Women have also been found to be more prone to nightmares than men. It is perhaps not surprising that feelings of helplessness, or of being threatened, are more common in women's dreams.

RIGHT *A detail of* Hell *from the* Garden of Earthly Delights *by Hieronymus Bosch (1450–1516). Bosch's paintings have an unnerving nightmarish quality.*

NIGHT TERRORS

These frightening feelings are caused by a sleep transmission disorder which occurs when the brain switches over from slow-wave sleep but doesn't fully complete the process. They are not really dreams as they don't occur during REM sleep. Neither do they feature strong visual images. However, they do provoke very strong physical reactions which can be alarming as the dreamer will awake from a night terror with a scream or shout, sit up in bed and look terrified. They will not remember much about the cause of their terror – just have a fleeting image in their mind accompanied by feelings of guilt, anxiety or shame.

HOW TO DEAL WITH NIGHTMARES

If stress and anxiety are the main causes of nightmares, it makes sense to try and reduce the stress levels in your life. Easier said than done, of course, but even practising simple relaxation techniques before going to sleep could help.

The best way to cope with dream fears is to confront them. One of the ways to do this is to think through your nightmare when you are awake, and rehearse it step by step. When it comes to the scary part – when the monster appears or an attack looms –

instead of running away, turn round and face it. Some therapists go even further and suggest that you not only stay put but actually fight back, either verbally or physically. The idea is that if you rehearse the confrontation in your waking life, you will prompt your memory so that you do the same when it happens in a dream.

Another way to confront the fear would be to re-run it over and over again, recording a description of the dream on tape or writing it down, then listening to or re-reading your account. This works on the premise that by continually confronting your fear you will eventually become familiar with it and therefore weaken its power.

Finally, you could appoint a dream guardian for protection. Think of a person or animal (it could be one you know or simply imagine), whom you could call upon to help you if you have a bad dream. Then imagine yourself back in the dream and call on your dream guardian for assistance. Tell yourself that the next time you have a bad dream your dream guardian will appear to help and protect you. As you fall

ABOVE *Try fighting back instead of running away from the monsters in your dreams.*

ABOVE *Practicing relaxation techniques before going to sleep can help to combat nightmares by reducing the anxiety and stress in your life.*

asleep, remind yourself that your guardian will be there if needed. This is a particularly useful and comforting technique to teach to children who suffer from nightmares.

RIGHT
Appoint a dream guardian to call on for protection when you are having a nightmare. This technique can be especially comforting for children. Painting by Alice Havers (1850–90).

Common Dream Themes

DREAMS ARE INDIVIDUALLY and uniquely ours, but there are certain themes and images common to all of us, irrespective of our background or culture, which crop up time and time again. These common themes, however, can only really be understood in the context of our own lives. A dream about falling, for example, may be an indication of feeling out of control, but to what extent will depend on what is happening in your life. The following are some of the dream themes we have probably all experienced at one time or another.

FLYING OR FLOATING

Dreams about flying commonly bring a feeling of freedom; they are seldom frightening or unpleasant, and the dreamer often awakes with a sense of optimism. The actual process of flying is usually effortless and the body feels weightless.

One of the most common explanations of a flying dream is that it represents a desire to "fly high" and an ability to cope with life, rising above it and viewing it from an objective standpoint. It could also indicate a love of risk-taking and adventure. If you are flying in a bed or an armchair (or even on a carpet), this suggests a desire for adventure but within the confines of comfort and security.

ABOVE *Flying dreams are usually exhilarating and optimistic. They can indicate a desire for adventure.*

BEING CHASED

A dream where you are being chased suggests you are running away from a situation that is threatening or frightening, or simply in danger of dominating the rest of your life. Perhaps there are problems that you are not facing, or obligations that need to be fulfilled.

ABOVE *Running away from a known, or unknown, adversary can mean that you are not facing up to problems in your waking life.*

This type of dream can also bring with it feelings of hopelessness and frustration because you are in a situation from which you feel you cannot escape. It may be worth looking at who is doing the chasing and what they represent. Is it a figure of authority, a father/mother figure, or something more scary and threatening? Another interpretation could be that whatever is chasing you is an aspect of yourself that you are afraid to confront.

FALLING

Whether it is falling from a cliff, a building or a wall, falling is a common dream theme that most of us will have experienced at some point. It has a number of meanings. It may signify feeling out of control or overwhelmed by a situation, such as the loss of a job or a divorce. Falling dreams also reflect a sense of having failed or "fallen down", so maybe you have tried to reach too high in your personal or professional life and fear that you are ready for a fall. Alternatively, the fall could symbolize a fear of "letting go".

Psychologists have speculated that fearful falling dreams are rooted in early childhood, when we learn to take our first steps. Some scientists have offered an interesting physiological explanation – that our muscles relax as we fall asleep and the falling sensation is actually the

ABOVE *Falling is a universal dream theme. It can mean a fear of "letting go" or indicates a sense of being overwhelmed.*

result of an involuntary muscle spasm, which then becomes incorporated into our dreams.

The old adage that if you hit the ground before waking up you will die cannot ever be proven. Who has died during such a dream and been able to recount it?

ABOVE *Drowning in your dream is clearly a symbol of anxiety in your waking life. But water can also represent a number of themes such as your emotions or the unconscious.*

LOSING TEETH

Whether they fall out all at once or slowly crumble, dreaming of losing teeth is very common and can be slightly alarming. Such a dream may reflect a number of deep seated fears such as a fear of ageing (and loss of sexual attractiveness), fear of losing power and control, or a fear of change. Biting or being bitten obviously symbolizes aggression!

LEFT *A dream about losing your teeth could indicate a deep seated fear or simply mean you are worried about a trip to the dentist!*

DROWNING

A dream about drowning could reflect an area in your life in which you are finding it difficult to "keep your head above water".

Large bodies of water are generally seen to represent the unconscious, so drowning could symbolize feeling engulfed by repressed, unconscious issues. Water is also a common symbol for the emotions, and dreams about drowning can happen during an emotional crisis or if you are feeling overwhelmed by your feelings.

LEFT *Sometimes in our dreams, we are faced with impending danger but find it impossible to run away.*

UNABLE TO MOVE

Being rooted to the spot but desperate to escape is a fairly classic anxiety dream. The physical paralysis could be a reflection of an emotional paralysis – perhaps you feel unable or reluctant to make changes in your life, or to make a decision, or maybe you are frustrated about a situation over which you feel you have no control.

BEING NAKED IN PUBLIC

The meaning of nakedness in dreams depends very much on how it feels.

If you feel embarrassed, ashamed and exposed, then this may reflect problems you have with feeling shy or socially inadequate. If, however, no-one seems to notice or care, it could mean that you are happy to reveal your "real self" to others. Nakedness can also represent the desire for freedom, or freedom of expression, reverting perhaps to our childhood innocence.

Being naked in a public place with others' disapproval could indicate that we are afraid of revealing our real selves.

LEFT *Being naked in a public place is a commonly occurring theme in our dreams. Its interpretation depends on our feelings and others' reaction.*

Dream Analysis

WHETHER YOU ARE experiencing troubled dreams which haunt your waking life, have a recurring dream that you would like to dispel, or just want to explore your dreams further, then dream therapy could be helpful.

Many schools of psychoanalysis use the study of dreams as part of their practice. This involves the patient talking about their dreams as a means to explore the unconscious and the thoughts, feelings and issues contained within. The dream is then looked at in relation to the patient's life. On a less complex level, there are some therapists who work solely with dreams. If you want to develop your own interpretive powers, you can attend dream workshops, in which techniques for dream analysis are taught, and dream groups in which people bring their own dreams for working on by the group as a whole.

The following are actual dreams which have been analysed by a psychoanalyst and dream therapist. Both were sent the narrative of the dream as well as some details of the dreamer and their situation at the time of the dream.

"FLYING TURTLES"

At the time of her dream, Kate was 27 years old and working as an administrator. She was considering giving up her job and changing careers.

ABOVE *Turtles have great symbolic and mythological significance.*

Kate is in a shallow pond with lots of people. They are in a race to row around the circumference of the pond. She begins the race in a boat, which then disappears and instead she is wading around in water. She feels very detached from the others. There are turtles of all different sizes swimming in the pond. The race has finished and everyone leaves the pond and walks up a path, the surface of which is covered with more turtles. Kate treads carefully, trying to avoid stepping on them, but she can feel some of the baby turtles getting crushed under her feet. She feels guilty about hurting them. Then suddenly they begin to grow wings, and fly away.

The analysis Water in dreams tends to signify the unconscious mind. Kate begins the race in a boat, which is a convenient way of travelling over water without being disturbed by it. It suggests something to do with her relationship with her unconscious, perhaps not being familiar with it, which is also indicated by the water's shallowness. The race is circular, with no beginning or end, which gives it a sense of futility and drudgery, and she is following the path of others. It is when Kate finds herself without a boat and wading through the water that she begins to feel detached from the other people.

The appearance of the turtles is a significant moment in the dream. As well as any personal significance or association they may have for Kate, turtles have a huge symbolic and mythological significance. In some cultures, they are believed to be divine. They often represent fertility and creativity, and turtles appear in numerous creation myths around the world.

Because of the creative significance of turtles, the dream is no doubt saying something about Kate's creativity, possibly a creative potential which hasn't yet been reached or realized. The turtles are also babies, so are symbolic of new life and potential. The fact that Kate walks on some of them potentially destroys the seeds of creativity, but they are not all destroyed and instead grow wings and fly away to safety, showing the potential for creative expression.

RIGHT *Water in dreams can signify the unconscious mind.*

"THE YELLOW DOG"

Sally, late 30s, is a designer. At the time of her dream, she was working hard to meet tight deadlines.

Sally is in a wide, tree-lined road with big, red-tiled houses set back from the street by long front gardens. There has been a flood, and a fast-flowing torrent is running down the middle of the road. Sally is being swept along by the current. She tries to grab hold of a tree trunk, and tries to cling on. There are no other people around but there is no sense of her having lost anyone. Suddenly, a large yellow labrador swims along. He holds his paw out in the air, leg outstretched, and says to her, "Hold on to me". He has managed to communicate without speaking – she doesn't hear any voice and his mouth hasn't moved. She holds on to his paw (he is big, strong and solid) and he gets her to safety, but she doesn't remember how. In the next scene of the dream, she is in a bar with a group of people who she doesn't know in real life but knows in her dream. The dog is still by her side, making sure that she's safe.

The analysis The setting represents affluence and stability, and could represent these aspects in Sally's life. The trees that line the wide road relate to family matters – trees are often linked to the family, hence the concept of the "family tree". The road symbolizes a direction in life. The flood and the strong current show that emotions are sweeping through any sense of stability that Sally may feel and are causing a huge

OPPOSITE *A flood or strong current in your dream can indicate sweeping emotions or a great upheaval in your waking life.*

upheaval. It is always better to go with the flow, rather than to try and swim against the current, but in her dream, Sally is resisting being swept away and wants to be rescued. Grabbing the tree shows that she is trying to feel grounded or "rooted".

ABOVE *A dog can represent faithfulness, loyalty, protection and rescue.*

The yellow labrador represents faithfulness and loyalty, protection and rescue. He could signify a real person and he may also represent intellect, as the colour yellow symbolizes intelligence. Perhaps Sally relies on her intellect, or rational side, to rescue her from emotional issues because she doesn't want her feelings to get in the way. Even in a social setting (a bar with people who are familiar in her dream but not actually known to her in her waking life) the dog is still there to protect her, so she feels she needs to use that part of her personality (her rational side) all the time.

Dream
Symbols

Dream Symbols

DREAMS USE THE LANGUAGE of metaphor and symbol to convey their meaning. Sometimes a symbol can be fairly straightforward, at other times it can be completely baffling. Some symbols are universal (the dove as a symbol of peace, the cross as a sign of Christ), but within the context of a dream even these mean different things to different people. The exact significance of a dream symbol is specific to each individual and his or her own experiences.

This list of symbols is intended as a springboard for your own interpretation. It is selective and by no means definitive – some symbols have just one interpretation, while others have a variety of possible meanings. Hopefully it will give guidance and spark off your own ideas and, in time, you may begin to develop your own list of dream symbols. Certain objects, people and situations may recur in your dreams and you will be able to attach your own meaning or significance to them.

The important thing to remember is that the feeling, tone and setting of a dream all have to be taken into consideration when you are exploring the possible meanings of symbols, and what they mean to you personally.

ANIMALS

Dog Animals signify our natural, instinctive and "animal" self. As domestic pets, dogs have a wide variety of symbolic meanings, including loyalty and companionship, going along with "the pack" and tamed wildness.

Cat Cats symbolize the feminine, sexuality, power and prosperity, and have both positive and negative connotations. They can be perceived as fertile and creative, but also "catty". A witch and a black cat generally stand for evil and bad luck.

Horse This powerful animal represents noble actions. It generally symbolizes mankind's harnessing of the wild forces of nature. If you are riding a horse in your

The horse can indicate noble actions.

dream, it could indicate that you are in control of your life. It could also represent your emotional state if the horse is running away with you, or you are reining it in.

A dog can symbolize loyalty.

A cat symbolizes female allure.

Bird Birds are complex symbols with a variety of meanings. They fly so they often represent physical or psychological freedom. They have a variety of religious meanings as messengers of the divine or symbols of the soul, and represent the "higher self" in most cultures. Blackbirds have traditionally been considered omens of death, as have carrion birds such as crows, ravens and vultures. The dove is a symbol of peace and reconciliation.

Birds are complex symbols.

A city has a very personal interpretation.

Fish Large areas of water represent the unconscious, so any creature living in water can represent a message or insight from the unconscious. Fish explore the depths of the ocean and are therefore positive symbols for anyone wanting to explore their own depths.

PLACES

Island Finding yourself on an island in a dream may mean that you need peace and solitude. It could also suggest that you are afraid of venturing into your unconscious mind (represented by the surrounding water) and prefer to stay on firm ground.

City The meaning of a city depends very much on your personal associations – whether or not you are a city-dweller, and whether you enjoy or dislike the urban environment. In Jungian psychology, the town or

city represents the community and social environment. If the city is busy and open, this could represent your relationships with other people. If it is chaotic and confused, this may symbolize how you are feeling. If you are lost in the city, this would probably represent a loss of direction in life. A ruined city may be an indication of neglected relationships or aims in life.

An island suggests peace.

A fish may signify an insight or message.

PEOPLE AND FIGURES

Baby A baby may represent a new beginning, development or opportunity. It can also represent your own "inner baby", the part of you that wants to feel secure and looked after.

Child A child could symbolize your own "inner child", the part that needs reassurance or needs to grow up. Dreaming of children can also symbolize a desire to go back to a more innocent, less complicated time in life. Like a baby, a child can also represent the possibility of a new beginning or new attitude to life.

Mother Symbolically, a mother represents giving life, love and nourishment. Being the mother in a dream denotes taking care of yourself or of a significant relationship in your life. The meaning

A baby can represent a new beginning.

of a dream about your own mother would depend entirely on your relationship with her, although the dream could be telling you something about that relationship.

Father The father figure represents power, authority, responsibility, caring and tradition. However, as with the mother figure, any

A father figure may symbolize caring or power.

interpretation of the appearance of your own father in a dream would depend entirely on your relationship with him.

Stranger In Freudian terms, meeting a stranger in a dream may symbolize meeting a part of one's own unconscious personality.

A child may represent our own "inner child".

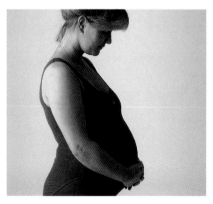

A mother can symbolize the giving of life.

A stranger could represent your unconscious personality.

A monster may represent repressed fears.

An actor can represent your "public" self.

An angel symbolizes purity and goodness.

Monster The appearance of a monster in a dream is usually caused by repressed emotions, anxieties and fears. It could also represent a part of your personality that you consider unpleasant or ugly and may try to keep hidden.

Giant A giant can be a friendly or scary symbol, either helpful and protective or terrifying. Because of its size, a giant could represent something large or overwhelming in the dreamer's life, a gigantic obstacle that needs to be overcome. The giant is also one of Jung's archetypes – part of the collective unconscious – and plays a large part in myth and legend.

Actor/actress Dreams in which you or others appear as actors tend to represent the public, rather than the private, self.

If it is an unpleasant dream about acting, it could refer to a situation or situations in which you feel forced to "put on an act" rather than being yourself.

Angel Traditionally seen as messengers of God, angels symbolize purity and goodness. They are also thought of as protectors and guides.

A giant can indicate a huge obstacle that needs to be overcome.

A house represents the dreamer.

Going back to school can symbolize nostalgia.

An opening can mean new opportunities.

HOUSES AND BUILDINGS

House A house is usually interpreted as representing the dreamer, with each room and floor representing a different aspect of the personality or mind. The living rooms represent the everyday, conscious life, the attic represents the higher, spiritual self, and the cellar represents the unconscious. The state of the house is also relevant. Is it dark and cramped, or light and airy? Does it need tidying? Do you get lost in it? Is it undergoing construction? Perhaps it is being decorated.

School A classroom typically represents learning but it can also represent competition or public esteem. Dreaming about being back in the classroom can indicate feelings of inadequacy, especially if the dream centres around unpleasant early school experiences. School can also symbolize nostalgia, expressing a desire to relive a feeling of ambition or joy from an earlier stage in your life.

An office may indicate professional standing.

Office If you dream about your own office, it may be an indication that you are bringing work home with you. An office can also symbolize authority or your position in the world.

Opening/doorway The meaning of a door or doorway depends entirely on how it appears in the dream. An open door could represent a new opportunity or phase in life, and going through the door would be to grasp that opportunity. Too many doors could suggest that a choice needs to be made. If the door is locked, it may indicate that something is being repressed or hidden

Prison A prison can be a sign that some part of you is being repressed and stifled, and needs to be released. Alternatively, it may be a sign that the dreamer needs to lock up certain actions or behaviour.

Tower A tower could be a symbol of caution and vigilance (a watchtower) or imprisonment (a guard tower). It could also be an ivory tower, representing arrogance and aloofness.

Hospital A hospital is a place for healing and getting back into the flow of life. It could also suggest that you may need to pay some attention to your health.

A prison may show that you feel stifled.

A tower could be a symbol of vigilance.

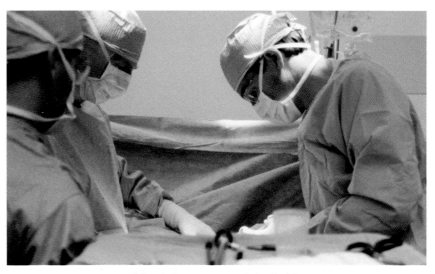

A hospital may mean you feel unhealthy.

TRAVEL

Station/airport Railway stations and airports represent many possibilities – a new venture or idea ready to "take off", apprehension or excitement about the future, or a transition in life. They can be confusing places, so their appearance in a dream may show that you need to sort through a particular problem or conflict.

Train A missed train could symbolize missed opportunities in life, as could being on the wrong train or missing a stop. Travelling smoothly down the track may mean staying "on track" in life. According to Freudian interpretation, the train represents the penis, and entering the tunnel (the vagina) represents sexual intercourse.

Car A car usually represents yourself and, in particular, whether or not you feel in control of your life. If you are "in the

A railway station may mean a new venture.

driver's seat", this may symbolize that you are taking charge of your life. If someone else is driving, it may show that you feel over-dependent on others, or are allowing others to control your life.

Road In dreams, roads represent a direction or goal in life. If the road is straight and narrow, you may be on the right path. If it is winding or bumpy, your

Roads symbolize a direction in life.

plans may be vague or have changed unexpectedly. If you never get to your destination, something could be preventing you from reaching your goal.

Aeroplane An aeroplane can be a positive symbol of liberation and freedom, particularly if you are the pilot and are able to "rise above" a situation or soar to new heights.

A train journey may mean you're "on track".

Driving a car may show you feel in control.

A flight can symbolize liberation.

BIRTH, MARRIAGE AND DEATH

Birth Birth can symbolize the beginning (actual or potential) of a new idea or project, or a sense of beginning a new stage in your life. Pregnant women often dream of difficult or strange births (for example, giving birth to kittens) which reflects their anxiety about childbirth.

Wedding/marriage Dreams of weddings or marriage can symbolize the union of opposite yet complementary parts of yourself, the most obvious being the union of the masculine and feminine parts of your personality.

Bride/bridegroom In Jungian psychology, dream images of a bride or bridegroom may represent the anima (feminine personality traits repressed in the male unconscious) in men, and the animus (masculine personality traits repressed in

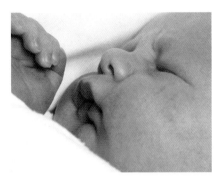

Giving birth may symbolize a new beginning.

the female unconscious) in women. Brides also traditionally symbolize purity and innocence.

Sex This is a complex area with a broad range of possible meanings that depend on the individual. Generally, seeing others having sex in a dream or having sex yourself could be simply an expression of sexual desire, a release of sexual tension,

a desire to bond, or an indication of repressed desires for physical and emotional love. Dreaming about sex with someone "inappropriate", or a person from your past, does not necessarily mean you harbour secret desires – your memory of them may have been triggered, or you may have come into contact with them recently.

Death Dreams about death or dying are not usually seen literally as omens of death, although they could express some anxiety about dying. Symbolically, death represents not so much an ending as a new beginning, so to dream of your own death could mean that you are preparing to start something new and are letting go of the old. If you dream of the death of a loved one, you may be rehearsing the actual event and unconsciously preparing yourself for bereavement.

Masculine and feminine combine in marriage.

Sex in dreams is a complex area.

Death in dreams is not usually a bad sign.

AGGRESSION AND VIOLENCE

Accident Being involved in an accident or crash in a dream could be a straightforward fear of being physically harmed. It may also suggest that you are in a state of anxiety, or even fear, that you are heading for an emotional "crash" or collision. If the general feeling of the dream is positive, although violent, it could symbolize a part of your life that you are letting go.

Accidents may show a fear of being harmed.

Violence towards others Horrifying scenes of violence or destruction may represent an overwhelming fear of the loss of your sense of power and control. If you are the one being violent, this could represent a struggle for self-assertion, or be an expression of a deep-rooted anger and resentment against some unwanted aspects of your life. Murder is a symbol of aggression and repressed rage at either the self or others. If the experience of violence leaves you feeling strangely neutral, as can sometimes happen in this kind of dream, physical violence could be a metaphor for another kind of conflict, maybe of opinions or ideas.

Violence towards oneself Directed at you (rather than inflicted by you), violence often represents a sense of guilt and a desire for self-punishment. It is also an indication that you are feeling vulnerable and battered by the outside world. Being a victim in a dream, or seeing another person being victimized, may represent a situation about which you feel helpless.

If you are violent towards others it can mean a desire for self-assertion.

Violence towards oneself can mean you are feeling helpless.

Examinations can stand for success or failure.

A bed may show a desire for escape.

Mirror A classic identity crisis dream is one in which you look into a mirror and see someone else's face. The face reflected may give you a clue to the nature of the identity problem. A cracked or clouded mirror reflects the distorted face (or image) you may be presenting to the world.

ANXIOUS SITUATIONS

Tests and exams In dreams, tests can stand for success or a fear of failure in your personal or professional life. Taking a test for which you have not prepared is a classic fear-of-failure dream. Passing an exam or test could be a metaphor for having succeeded in something.

Interviews Having an interview can show anxiety. The people on the interview panel could represent aspects of the dreamer's self image – perhaps dissatisfaction or judgement.

Interviews are common anxiety dreams.

OBJECTS

Bed A bed can be a symbol of security, warmth and comfort, maybe even of escaping from the outside world. If a bed appears in a dream about marriage or a relationship, then the state of the bed could be seen as representing the state of the relationship.

Book Books represent knowledge and wisdom, or the historical record of the dreamer's life. A dusty old book could symbolize forgotten or neglected knowledge, or an earlier "chapter" of your life. The opening and closing of a book may represent the relevant "chapter" of your life.

Books can symbolize wisdom.

Clock/watch In dreams, clocks often reflect anxiety about not being on top of things or being behind schedule. They may also symbolize your emotions.

Clocks can reflect anxieties.

A body of water represents the unconscious.

The pace of a river's flow may be significant.

Fire can mean passion or danger.

NATURE AND THE ELEMENTS

Sea Large bodies of water generally represent the unconscious and the emotions within it, so feelings about the sea in a dream could indicate your emotional state. Are you feeling lost in a small boat, or safe and protected in a large one? Is the water calm or are you feeling overwhelmed by huge waves? Are you afraid of monsters that lurk in the dark waters? Because the sea can mean all of these things, it is particularly important to take note of the emotional atmosphere of the dream.

River As with the sea, a river is a large body of water and generally represents an emotional state. Watching a river flow passively may indicate that life is passing you by without enough direction. If the river is bursting its banks and over-flowing, this may reflect a feeling of being out of control. Crossing a river by a bridge may symbolize that you are undergoing a change in life, or it may mean that you are avoiding a flood of passion by observing the water from a safe position.

Fire This element is a complex symbol which has many different meanings, including passion, anger, illumination and danger. Fire can purge as well as consume, purify as well as destroy. An out-of-control fire could be a sign of unbridled passion or ambition.

A mountain is usually positive.

The flower is a symbol of fragility.

A steep slope may show a lack of progress.

An avalanche shows we are overwhelmed.

Flower The flower in your dreams is a natural symbol of beauty, fragility and harmlessness. It can also symbolize the attraction of bees to nectar. In Asian yoga teachings, flowers represent the psychic centres or "chakras" on which to focus meditation practice.

Mountain Climbing a mountain and reaching the top could be a positive symbol that you are achieving your goals. Surveying the landscape from the top of a mountain could represent looking at life objectively, or assessing it without any emotional attachment. Descending a mountain could mean that you are letting go of insurmountable issues.

Slope Trying to ascend a slippery slope is a common dream which suggests that you are failing to progress in a certain area of your waking life. Stumbling or slipping down the slope may signify that you are forcing yourself to do things which go against your nature.

Forest Commonly an element of fairy tales and legends, a forest is a symbol of the unconscious, so venturing into a forest can be seen as an exploration of the unconscious mind. A forest can also represent a refuge from the demands of everyday life.

Avalanche An avalanche signifies being overwhelmed or fearing disaster. It may also symbolize "frozen" emotions that should be expressed or experienced.

A forest is a classic part of fairy tales and myths and symbolizes the unconscious.

Index

The publishers would like to thank the following picture libraries and photographers for the use of their pictures in the book:

AKG London: 10bl; 15bl; 16l; 18; 21tr; 30; 36; 37br; 38. Ancient Art & Architecture: 11; 12tr; 13t, b. The Art Archive: 12l; 15tr; 23; 39r. Bridgeman Art Library: 8tr; 9; 10tr; 17; 28; 41r. Fine Art Photographic Library: 8br; 22br; 55bl. Images Colour Library: 21bl; 33tr; 60t; 63tr. Stone Images: 14t, b; 16r; 20bl; 25tr; 32tr; 33tl; 39tl; 56tl, tr; 58bl; 60bl; 61br. SuperStock: 34tr; 55tm, tr, tl; 58bm; 60br.